Ministry and Parenting Challenges

Gracia Kasanda Mubala

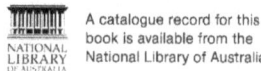 A catalogue record for this book is available from the National Library of Australia

Copyright © 2020 Gracia Kasanda Mubala
All rights reserved.
ISBN: 978-1-922343-37-6

Linellen Press
265 Boomerang Road
Oldbury, Western Australia
www.linellenpress.com.au

Dedication

I dedicate this book to The Kasanda's family for the labour put into ministry for the glory of God.

Contents

Dedication iii
Contents v
Acknowledgments vii
Overview 1
Introduction 5
Getting Started 7
Why does the cost of ministry affect families … 9
Ministry with Children 13
Ages 0 to 18 13
Be a Realistic Person and Parent 20
But a child who understands … 26
Am I bound to be in ministry … ? 29
Support from a child who understands 31
It's never too late to start Amendments 33
Conclusion 35
About the Author 36

Acknowledgments

I acknowledge my parents, Pastor Luc Kasanda, the teacher of the Word, along with my mother, a strong and grounded woman.

I acknowledge my siblings Noela, Nadege and Heritier for allowing God to still use them despite the challenges we faced growing up as P. Ks (Pastor's Kids).

Overview

I am inspired to write this book because, being a Pastor's daughter, I have an insight into what goes on in many ministerial families, both close and far. This book is not to criticize Pastors but to help Christian leaders improve their lifestyle and warn those who are to enter a full-time ministry of the challenges ahead of them so that they can overcome them. All to the glory of our God, who called us according to His purpose.

Below is what Bishop Sam Dako said.

A Pastor's life!

The lawyer, the lecturer, the journalist, the doctor, the pharmacist, the pilot is 'working'. But many think the pastor is playing and needs a real JOB!

People think everyone else in every other profession is really busy, but when it's a pastor, they say "Go and look for a job." Well done. People applaud professions that help people and a pastor's role is no less important than the lawyer, doctor, or nurse.

Footballers earn far more than doctors, Comedians earn far more than teachers. Most pastors earn very little, or nothing, and you think that's fine? How has Messi helped people's lives and given them new hope for a living? Or, how has Basketmouth (comedian) saved people's marriages or helped deliver people from addiction?

Pastors are involved daily, bearing the brunts of helping people live a better life, and yet, when people see them own a few things, they behave as though they don't deserve anything.

"In case you don't know, being a pastor is one of the most demanding and sacrificial jobs I know on earth," Bishop Sam Dako said.

"I have been a pastor for the past 26 years now. I have been to police stations … several because of church members. I have visited several hospitals and spent nights there awake because of church members. I have traveled long distances, given up belongings, attended to marriages on the verge of divorce, and conducted funerals all because of church members. The last was a family, who was barely four months in the church, who had an accident. The woman and her baby died on the spot. When I got there, their whole family was crying to me, asking me in tears, "Pastor Why?"

"Who else is supposed to answer such a question? It's always the pastor. Yet, in the midst of that, we bring courage and restore hope. But when it comes to a pastor having money, people will frown, and wag their tongue against it. And yet the economy is not different for pastors! Everyone else cries, but when a pastor does, he has no Faith. Everyone can bring their problems to the pastor, but no one asks if the pastor has eaten, he should tell it to God."

Pastor Sam Dako's words express what a lot of pastors go through to serve God.

Introduction

This book intends to give an insight into what goes on in most but not all pastoral/ minister's families so that corrections may be made. It is also a precaution for parents and families who are new into ministry. There are many challenges that pastors face as parents and families, but the negative impacts of these challenges are more significant on their children. The topics discussed also include why the cost of ministry has a significant effect on families.

This book gives an insight into the challenges and how pastoral families, new and old, can correct their wrongs regardless of how they've allowed these challenges to destroy their relationships within families and be more vigilant to the devices of the enemy.

Getting Started

Ministry, particularly Christian ministry, is the archetype of being in the "GREAT COMMISSION" to direct church members and sometimes non-church members.

There are many posts or callings in the Christian Faith. Some are called:

- Apostles, Prophets, Pastors, Teachers and so forth – in these include church planting, individual/group discipleship, just to mention a few
- Worshippers, (choir leaders), ushers, intercessors, media, and so forth.

The ministries mentioned above come at a high cost, and the effect of these costs is more significant on families.

Luke 14:26 'if anyone comes to me and does not hate his father, mother, wife, children, brothers, and sisters – yes even their own life such a person cannot be my disciple".

Yes, Jesus said to hate our father, mother, wife, brothers, and sister, but what He actually meant is we need to be willing to give up whatever it takes in order to be His disciples. We need to follow where He leads us. If at any point our parents, brothers, sisters, wives, husband, or anyone, gives us thoughts, opinions or advice that is against the word of God, or our God given assignment then we have to make the hard decisions to stand firm and obey Our Lord Jesus and the Holy Spirit.

Why does the cost of ministry affect families the most?

Ministry is not a bad thing at all. In fact, it is the best and most rewarding job on earth, and in heaven. Winning souls for Christ, healing the sick, restoring marriages, and so forth is the best job to have. Paul instructed Timothy in 1 Timothy 3 saying:

"If anyone wants to provide leadership in the church, good! But there are preconditions: A leader must be well-thought-of, committed to his wife, cool and collected, accessible, and hospitable. He must know what he's talking about, not be over-fond of wine, not pushy but gentle, not thin-skinned, not money-hungry. He must handle his own affairs well, attentive to his own children, and having their respect. For if someone is unable to handle his own affairs, how can he take care of God's church?"

Today's pastoral or families under minsters face a high level of neglect and isolation from parents. The instructions that Paul gave to Timothy regarding leadership in the church were to ensure that, as we step up into the office of the ministry, we must not forget our first assignment as a person, child of God, and as parents.

The costs in church leaders' lives, particularly pastors, bishops, apostles, and their families include:

- ➢ Lack of family time
- ➢ Emotionally left out for the children
- ➢ Not there for the wife or children (in some circumstances) when needed
- ➢ The cost of living due to extra church expenses for new small church or less committed givers.
- ➢ Insults

There are a lot of them. The mistake most pastors make, especially the ones who shepherd a church is that once they are devoted, they are **devoted,** putting the needs of wives and children aside. Family becomes a stumbling block when the wife and children start to demand attention.

In some cultures, like eastern and African cultures, tradition says the wife and children have little or no say at all. It is the parents' right to be respected, which is not bad. However, in most cases, children tend not to respect their parents because parents should earn their respect, not expect it through fear and intimidation. I thank God that today's generation's mentality is adapting to change. Nevertheless, these things still happen in most families. I am standing as a voice to speak for those who are still living under this bondage.

The first ministry for a married man and woman is family. I had an opportunity to chat with a former police officer and his wife, former teachers who are now foster parents. I will never forget what they told me. They said, "Before I consider becoming a foster parent, I have to make sure *my* children are well natured, mature enough and know where they stand in the family." Talking from experience, they had made that mistake years back and decided to repair it before it was too late. I don't think these people are born again from their lifestyle, but using them as an example, if we, the earthly parents, know how to give good things to *our* children how much more will God give those who are his children, expressing the godly nature of love, mercy, understanding and so forth? If it happens that a time when we are called in ministry while our children are very young, it is highly recommended that parents in this post should consider the children in the process.

Schedule time for family – believe you me, there's time for everything.

My father became a Pastor before I was born. Can you imagine the transition of being a devoted pastor to a married man, and then having children?

God knows we are seasonal beings, and He is also a God of families. There was a time when my parents had to ensure that we ate before they could travel for ministry. And now that all the girls are grown up, and are all married, they can and have all the time they need to travel. In times like this, it's easier for them to go everywhere God will send them with no restrictions.

Ministry with Children
Ages 0 to 18

Ministers with children aged 0 to 14 face a lot of challenges, because it is a crucial time in their lives. The best time to invest in your children is when they are young. When the foundation is faulty, what can a righteous do? When we neglect our children, we pay the price. Some negligent acts can cost the lives of our children. We may not be around anymore, but the child will still carry the scars of those acts throughout their lifetime. *Ouch*!! A lot comes out of sleepovers, leaving children with any church member without discernment. But some of the people we leave our children with are not really established in the Lord.

It becomes more difficult when a pastor doesn't hear from the Lord. From experience, it's not that they don't hear from the Lord. They still do not hear enough from Him. Once they start making a name, God starts to elevate them; they begin to rely on their own strength to build and maintain a good reputation.

When I was in my first or second year of university, I received this revelation. When a soldier is sent on a mission, they are given telecommunication devices to communicate with those who sent them out in the field. When a satellite or connection is lost, the soldier will be in trouble. So, if they don't hear from the Lord, then how do they know they are being called on to start a church? Through prophecy from another pastor? Come on!!

When this happens, some pastors start to put more effort in leading the church, and their families are the ones who pay the price. When children are young, this is the time for training with lots of corrections, love, attention, care, and nurturing. If you invest wisely, they will be easier to mentor when they reach their teen years and move into their adulthood.

Unfortunately, many relationships between parents and children have gaps in these two stages. Then later, when the children grow older, it definitely backfires and the children and parents drift apart. That is why we see pastors' children getting influenced by the world when they start high school. They see other children and envy the attention they get from their parents.

In some cases, it's not just the children who miss out, but wives too. As the husbands are devoted, they don't bring their wives along in spiritual growth. Lack of spiritual growth for a spouse is a big dilemma in ministry. The wife is forced to labour for her children, and therefore doesn't have time to mentor her children, answer their questions because she is frustrated and bitter. A bitter mother is a dangerous mother. Out of this, some die of stress. High blood pressure kicks in. And some end up divorcing because the husband is never there, or she feels so neglected by her husband that she loses herself in the process.

These negative occasions open evil doors. For example, when a husband (the pastor) sees a more composed sister than his wife, single mum or not, he'll fall for her. He'll defend himself that he has found "mwasi ya minister," meaning I have found a ministry wife (a common phrase used in Lingala). What a shame! All this happens because there's no time for each other as husband and wife.

1 Corinthians 7: 5 Paul says:

Marriage is a decision to serve the other, whether in bed or out. Abstaining from sex is permissible for a period of time if you both agree to it and if it's for the purpose of prayer and fasting – but only for such times. Then come back together again. Satan has an ingenious way of tempting us when we least expect it.

"The marriage bed must be a place of mutuality –the husband seeking to satisfy his wife, the wife seeking to satisfy her husband. Marriage is not a place to "stand up for your rights."

In ministry, especially preachers, we know the bible. We know God's instruction, but why do we still fall?

Please allow me to open a bracket with this scripture.

2 Thessalonian 1: 11 "wherefore also we pray always for you, that our God would count you worthy of this calling, and fulfill all the good pleasure of his goodness, and the work of faith with power" (KJV).

I came across this scripture in my quiet time. During bible study with a woman of God I respect so much, she instructed me to pray for people who were very close to me on the wings of this scripture. Why pray for God to be counted as worthy of this calling? Whatever your calling is. It's because many start well, with good intentions. But things happen along the way that makes some divert from good intentions to evil. From a humble heart to fame; from true service to preaching for sustenance. Others out of ignorance move from Faith to feelings. To avoid this, we need to be in a constant relationship with the father. This will help us follow the equation of God, which is:

> *Instruction*
>
> *+ Action – obedience/disobedience*
>
> *= Blessings or Punishment*

When we apply the word of God in our homes, in this case, applying Paul's advice to handle our own affairs well, we are being attentive to managing our home well.

As church leaders, we may speak well outside but we need to apply what we preach. A pastor's daughter once said to me that we need to be careful with our children because they are the ones who know us in depth. She was referring to ministers, pastors whose children are well under them, not yet at the point of leaving home. Why did she say this? If, for example, I as a choir leader or intercessor gossip in front of my children, speaking evil against other choir members, and not live for God in my home and behind closed doors, I am planting a bad seed in them. These actions also give children a bad image that it is impossible to live for God.

I once said to myself when I was 19 years old that I didn't want to get married to a pastor. I still prayed for a godly man, a man who's not into the affairs of the world, but not a pastor. One of my young sister's really didn't want to marry a pastor … but guess what? She's a pastor's wife!! Not funny, but God knows the beginning and the end of our lives. We are all married to people God has chosen from the field he has chosen them. What made her say that? It's because our lives were a sacrifice in service, especially migrating to Australia. We were very young – not knowing why we did it (anyway) was the biggest challenge. It has many benefits to serve the Lord. I have many testimonies that show how some pastors mentor their children well, and they turn out well while others who mentor their congregation first, their children turn out not so well.

I am not saying that pastors should let their children live their lives like they are not pastors' children. What I am saying here is that consider your children. Be their mentor. Seat them down and tell them why you are in ministry, why you do it. Why they should be involved.

Be a Realistic Person and Parent

Jesus said in John 5:19-23,

"then Jesus answered and said to them, "Most assuredly, I say to you, the Son can do nothing of Himself, but what He sees the Father do; for whatever He does, the Son also does in like manner.

20 For the Father loves the Son, and shows Him all things that He Himself does; and He will show Him greater works than these, that you may marvel.

21 For as the Father raises the dead and gives life to them, even so the Son gives life to whom He will.

22 For the Father judges no one, but has committed all judgment to the Son,

23 that all should honor the Son just as they honor the Father. He who does not honor the Son does not honor the Father who sent Him.

This scripture tells me that a leader, be it a father, brother, pastor or similar has the responsibility to show his followers how to do God's work, ministry, and so on. Parents are the primary and best leaders children could ever learn from. Therefore, we have to be mindful of what we teach and do in front of our children. If people do not honor me as a pastor's child that means there's something they see in me that makes them act the way they do. If they do it out of jealousy, hatred or are satanic agents, that's another issue altogether.

Titus 2:1-8, for the sake of the Gospel, Paul tells Titus to teach sound doctrine, giving the older men and women instructions on how to live so that they can urge the younger women and encourage the young men to do the right things. Our followers learn from the good examples of our leaders and, most importantly, from what they see! What they learn is what they'll pass on to the next generations. If it's bad, it will only take God's mercy to deliver and break that flow. Children are wiser than we think.

Children see some things but may not be able to express themselves for one reason or another. Some unanswered question are retained within them and when the time comes, they'll start discussing it with their friends. When they have carried enough in their hearts, it will overflow whether you are the biggest controlling mother or not. I don't want to go into details but, truly speaking, there are parents who are in denial of reality. And when something happens, they explore to the point of devouring and disowning their children. Then where is the GOSPEL you are preaching as the pastor, spiritual and biological parent?

If a parent, especially in ministry, doesn't pay attention to their actions, their actions will pay attention to them and will surely work against the one day. The blame will be on the parent both from other people and their own children. This hurts more because inasmuch as the parent's mind would be in denial, the conscious will judge. So, teach what you apply. Ministers with families, spouse and ministers' children can confirm this to be true or not. If those around a pastor or minister of God don't see them apply what they preach, it makes it harder for them to accept the teachings of the pastor.

The same applies to a minister's family. When the pastor is busy preaching about respecting wives when he himself calls his wife names, or a wife who constantly preaches submission when she is not submissive, makes it harder for the spouse to believe what the wife preaches. If you give each other attention as a family, you will earn each other's respect. When the right attention is given to young children and teenagers, the problems families face will diminish. When a pastor mentors his son and teaches him how to deal with stress, how to overcome teenage blues, and all that, families won't have to deal with pregnancy before marriage, rebellion or falling into all kinds of temptation.

There's a saying that "you only gave birth to a child, not the child's heart". This means that you give birth to a child, you don't give birth to their interest, ideas, inspiration etc.

First and for most, children are a gift from the Lord.

Psalms 127:3. Our children belong to the Lord. God has just entrusted us with the children we have. Some of us get the privilege to raise our children. So, as a parent, do not have a mentality that we own our children. When I receive a gift from someone, I am happy and I will value that gift because it is an honor to receive that gift. Some gifts are more expensive than what we can personally afford. Parents reading this book, if I were to ask you this question, 'how much does your child worth?' I don't know your answer but, will leave you to answer that question. Why and How do we get from a point of enjoying our gift (s) to a point of owning our children?

Train your child in the way he or she should go. Tell them the truth about life. Don't lose them along the way. The neglect leads to pain. Yes, we may not have it all but through that children also learn that there's life beyond not having it all.

Some pastor's children have suffered in the hands of church members, from being called names, for any mistakes they make, or even just having a better house or more money than them. That should be something you sit your children down and mentor them.

Leaving children to anyone has cost many pastors' children their virginity, innocence, trust, and much more. I am not making us feel bad about full-time ministry but just to wake us up. Inasmuch as we are under God's protection, we are also called to be *as wise a serpent and harmless as a dove,* **Matthew 10:16**.

I don't want to talk much on this but know that the devil is at work. If he can't get you on a particular weakness, he will want to intrude into your home because he knows it will hurt you the most when your children leave the church you are pastoring, or if they commit a shameful act. To you, firstly as a parent is shameful, secondly as a minister it's twice as shameful, and it brings blasphemy to the body of Christ. If we can take a step back as ministers, sit down and talk to our children we will have averted avoidable wrongs.

But a child who understands that the rules are for their own good will be in a good perspective

This is just a word of advice: if you have intentions of handing over ministry to your children then you have to prepare them for ministry. I have firsthand instances of a minister parent/guardian who does not praise their children, but are very good at telling others to praise their children. Tears just fill up when I see this occur. But it is a good lesson to me as well.

Be extra attentive to your children and bring them along in ministry. Let them travel with you if time allows. Take time to tell them why you are in ministry, and don't be afraid to tell them where you have failed … with wisdom and depending on their maturity. Beware of what's going on in your children's lives. Can they confide in you without regretting taking such a bold step as to tell you what is really going on? Just as we encourage church members and those we are winning to Christ to confess their sins, do it the same way for our children.

Remember we are not fighting against flesh and blood but against powers, high-rank spiritual rulers, and principalities. If you are residing in the country of your origin, it is to your advantage because you know what fights and challenges children in your country have. Coming from Congo DR., I have heard testimonies of the Spiritual government in Congo. Those in Power can't allow policies or roads to be put in place if the spiritual government does not approve it. It doesn't matter if the Congolese earthly government approves it. So, you can help your children overcome these challenges by prayer. Pray for them, pray with them, build a rapport with them. Show them the way of God.

Don't play gigi-gigi- From experience some parents expect 100 percent Holiness from their children with no mercy. No room for mistakes, and that is very dangerous. For instance, there's a difference between someone who is passionate about their role in a business and the one who's not. The passionate one believes in pushing the company forward but the other just wants their paycheck and go to pay bills. Such people will just obey the rules so they don't get in trouble (e.g. children) but discussing the rules with children will create the opportunity to build a good relationship between parents and children.

Reminder: Minister's children also fight our battles. These children are innocent, especially when they are born to parents who started ministry before they were born, or when they are very young. Apart from attacking families, Satan and his agents attack ministers' children and families to destabilise them. So, if you take anything or everything your teenage child or adult does as dishonour, shame, or disobedience, think again. Not all is a child's desire to disrespect you. Some of us endured till we burnt out. No one to talk to, no one to understand you, and also being careful of the people who do not keep confidences. Confidence taken away, they become too quiet as a result of isolation and bitterness. Others interpret it as being too proud that he or she is born into a pastoral family. If not for the Holy Ghost, only God knows.

Am I bound to be in ministry because I was born in a ministerial or pastoral Family?

First of all, Jeremiah 1: 5 says,

"Before I formed you in the womb, I knew you, and before you were born, I consecrated you; I appointed you a prophet of many nations. Galatians 1:15 & 16. "But He who had set me apart before I was born and He who called me by His grace so I say walk by the Spirit and you will not gratify the desires of the flesh".

Whoever desires ministry desires a good thing according to Paul in 1 Timothy 3:1. Sometimes parents want to impose children to take up a particular ministry post, for instance, as on the pastoral post when the child is called to feed the poor or be a worshipper.

Before imposing anything, please consult with the Holy Spirit lest you interfere in God's plan and ruin your child's destiny. So, train a child in a godly way so that when time comes, both of you will consult the Holy Spirit and not impose anything on each other. To children, I encourage you to read Proverbs 6. Our parents are more experienced than us. In some matters, consider their wise advice.

Support from a child who understands

Often parents want their children to support them either in ministry, business, or to be their successor. My husband said to me that I couldn't just buy a house or take my business and give it to my child as an inheritance. Not that it's a bad thing but, without teaching that child the value of the business, the downfall of that business is higher. In saying this, inasmuch as we want our children to support us, it is also essential to spend quality time with your children. Spend one-on-one time with each child and collectively. This will help parents have an idea of what their children's goals and desires are. At times as parents we know what's right for our children, but if we impose it, it may backfire and we end up hurt. The child is also hurt and feels that he or she is not loved enough to express their desires.

Thank God for Bible studies, Apostle Isaiah talked about the four cognitive stages of child developments, by Jean Piaget. These stages are important to help parents shape a child for a better end for both parents and children, because they will help you make a better vision of raising your children.

They say Charity begins at home. When a child has not shown interest in what you want them to be involved in from day one, and as a parent does little or nothing about it, when a child grows, you will need divine intervention to get your child to do what you want. So, allow your children to freely express themselves as they get older and correct them along the way. Address issues as they rise, of course, with respect. I learnt that parents need to communicate with Love, and children need to communicate to their parents with respect, even if respect in different cultures differs. So, parents start from a young age, teaching children and letting them know their expectations.

It's never too late to start Amendments

If a family has totally broken down, thank God for whoever and whatever you still have. First, forgive yourself. Forgive one another. Make peace and move on. Cut off strings attached to our help. Personal experience, my husband and I had reached a point where we didn't accept help anymore because there were strings attached to most of the help we received. That was, and still is, getting in the way of those who genuinely want to help.

Peace cannot be made if deceit is involved, or twisting the matter and making assumptions. There's a cartoon of the Jehovah's witness called Caleb and Sophia. I loved showing the younger version to my children because at least it is morally teaching family time of reading the bible and praying together and other things like 'obey your parents', 'sharing' etc. One day, I stumbled on the grownup's version and my soul grieved. Sophia complained of being molested by a deacon in the church but her parents didn't listen to her and that changed her life negatively. Caleb was now a drunkard. Caleb and Sophia turned out to be the opposite of what they were taught as kids, leaving their mother on anti-depression medication and their dad an alcoholic. In short, for me, my first ministry is my children because, when they are taught and grounded in God, God will reward me as their parent and God will take care of the evil attacks from the outside world.

As a minister, I don't want to be empty. As a minister, don't focus more on the outside because if you are empty on the inside, you don't have anything to impact lives with. If we confess that we are children of God, ministers, pastors, and worshippers, let us be honest, we can look good outside but what profits a man to gain the world and lose his soul? Don't do it just for people, do it for God. What will people say if my children leave the church I'm pastoring? What will people say that my daughter fell pregnant? And yes, it's shameful and all that, but during that time, instead, redeem your daughter. Don't punish your son or daughter to the point you can't repair them and pretend all is good. It hurts more when it's your parents or guardian that's doing this, and your friends outside are comforting you.

Conclusion

In conclusion, it is not wrong to desire ministry. However, create a balance between ministry and family.

Seek God's face regarding His calling upon your children and direct them with Love as Paul said in 1 Timothy 3.

As parents, we also need to seek God's face regarding God's calling upon our children.

Work with our children by communicating in a way that will benefit both parents and children to build one another in Love and Unity.

More Grace to every minister and P.Ks out there.

About the Author

Originally from Congo DR, Gracia moved from Zambia to Australia in 2006. Gracia is the mother of three beautiful children who, with her husband, devotes her time to the family and the ministry. Having grown up as a pastor's daughter, she maintains important family values and strong relationships with her children, while serving the ministry and the Lord.

In Church, Gracia sings in the choir and plays the keyboard. She has studied Commerce, Counselling and Community Services, which enabled her to write this, her first, book.

Gracia is also the author of *Seasons Come and Go, But God Never Changes*.

www.ingramcontent.com/pod-product-compliance
Lightning Source LLC
Chambersburg PA
CBHW071548080526
44588CB00011B/1832